# Clara and the Crystal Christmas Tree!

## Written by Amy-Lee Campbell
### Illustrated by Moli_art

To all the amazing women and wonderful little girls that I have in my life. I love you! Thank you for your inspiration!

I am embracing, acknowledging and appreciating the gifts of Clair Senses today and always.

~Amy-Lee

# This book belongs to:

_____

# Clara and the Crystal Christmas Tree!

One winter's morning, the snow was gently falling, and Clara knew Christmas Day would soon be coming.

She spoke with her parents and told
them she was starting to worry.
Their Christmas tree had no decorations
yet, and she wanted to finish in a hurry.

Their family had moved homes in the
early part of spring.
Now they couldn't find their Christmas
decorations, not a single thing.

Clara and her family searched their
home high and low.
They found the lights, and their
excitement began to grow.

10

That evening they added the lights to the tree, but something was still missing. Those decorations, where could they be?

With a hot chocolate and cookies, Clara went to her room.
She thought to herself, I must make my own decorations. Christmas will be here soon!

14

Clara looked around her room and saw her crystal collection of plenty and thought, I'll craft some crystal decorations. I have so many!

She worked very hard and crafted lots of
crystal ornaments.
Big, small, and colorful, they were of all
different assortments.

18

The next day as the family placed the crystals on the tree, the family was so grateful, and Clara was as proud as could be!

20

Crafting crystals for Christmas was a beautiful addition. So now Clara and her family made it their Christmas tradition.

22

# Merry Christmas!

# The End

Made in the USA
Columbia, SC
30 November 2022

72396996R00018